MIDDLE NEIGHBORHOODS

ACTION AGENDA FOR A NATIONAL MOVEMENT

Project Director: Paul C. Brophy

Summary Report Prepared by Paul C. Brophy,
Pamela Puchalski, and Stephanie Sung

IN PARTNERSHIP WITH

WITH SUPPORT FROM

BLE OF CONTENTS

PREFACE

David H. Mortimer
President
The American Assembly

In 2016, as part of its ongoing work to strengthen U.S. cities, The Ameri
Assembly of Columbia University initiated an investigation into mic
neighborhoods—communities "on the edge" between success and declin
which was directed by Paul C. Brophy, a leading expert on affordable housing
community development. This included the publication of *On the Edge: Amer*
Middle Neighborhoods with the Federal Reserve Bank of San Francisco. In a se
of case studies and essays by leading policymakers, community developn
professionals, and scholars, *On the Edge* identifies and explores the complex
of communities transitioning—for better or worse—across America. Follov
the book's publication, The American Assembly organized convenings in ci
across the United States to facilitate author presentations aimed at inforn
new audiences about these neighborhoods. These convenings were paired \
strategic meetings among elected officials, urban policy experts, commu
development practitioners, and researchers. The response across cities
at the national level was promising, as diverse stakeholders began to recog
the importance of this often-overlooked category of neighborhoods. Local
national media also started reporting on middle neighborhoods. Finally,
congressional briefing in May 2017, the issues under discussion included l
federal action might encourage more local investment to boost the econo
vitality of neighborhoods. With this base of interest and support, local
national advocates were brought together for a working meeting in Baltim
This report is the summary of that meeting.

On November 15–16, 2017, the fifty-four participants from government, law,
academia met with leaders of civic, philanthropic, and public policy organizati
in structured discussions examining policies, approaches, and strategies concern
middle neighborhoods poised between stability and distress. The Assembly

ed by the Lincoln Institute for Land Policy and Healthy Neighborhoods, Inc.
rganizing "Middle Neighborhoods: Action Agenda for a National Movement"
 the Federal Reserve Bank of Richmond at its Baltimore offices. Paul Brophy
ed as chair, and Pamela Puchalski, senior adviser to The Assembly, organized
 helped structure the event with the invaluable assistance from local groups
The Assembly's staff, Stephanie Sung and Mark Leneker.

participants were split into three working groups that focused broadly on
arch, practice, and policy. They also met in plenary sessions for presentations,
ussion, and a moderated panel. Baltimore Mayor Catherine E. Pugh welcomed
participants, and David Erickson, Director of Community Development of the
eral Reserve Bank of San Francisco moderated a panel with Councilwoman
relle Parker of Philadelphia; Johnette Richardson, Executive Director
Baltimore's Belair-Edison Neighborhoods; and Laura Gamble, President
Maryland Regional, PNC Financial Services. The participants also heard
entations about middle neighborhoods initiatives in their cities from Mark
nan, President, Healthy Neighborhoods, Inc., Baltimore; Nedra Sims Fears,
cutive Director, Greater Chatham Initiative, Chicago; Joel Ratner, President
 CEO, Cleveland Neighborhood Progress; and Jeffrey Verespej, Executive
ctor, Old Brooklyn Community Development Corporation in Cleveland.

strength of this report is due in large part to the co-chairs and rapporteurs
ach of the discussion groups: Alan Mallach, Todd Swanstrom, and Jesse
gan—Research; Nedra Sims Fears, Marcia Nedland, and Stephanie Sung—
tice; and Joe McNeely, Cherelle Parker, and Peter Dolkart—Policy. Without
r remarkable facilitation, the caliber of the discussions that informed this
rt simply could not have occurred.

are particularly grateful to the Muriel F. Siebert Foundation, PNC Financial
ices, and Lincoln Institute of Land Policy whose generous support permitted the
ting to take place.

LAIMER

report is a summary of the issues and priorities discussed among the working
ps in individual and plenary sessions, at the "Middle Neighborhoods:
on Agenda for a National Movement" meeting on November 15–16, 2017
Baltimore, MD. While the working group co-chairs and rapporteurs edited
 report, the individual participants did not. The participation of those who
ently serve in a policymaking position should not be taken as an endorsement
he views or recommendations herein.

Belair-Edison neighborhood, Baltimore. Photo credit: Belair-Edison, Inc.

MIDDLE NEIGHBORHOODS

Middle neighborhoods are among the most racially and socioeconomically diverse neighborhoods in the nation.

y-eight percent of urban residents in the United States live in middle hborhoods. Middle neighborhoods are among the most racially and economically diverse neighborhoods in the nation, and many are threatened decline or gentrification, depending on the market conditions in their unding cities and suburbs. This key fact was the reason fifty-four experts met altimore in mid-November 2017 as part of a three-part agenda to protect the ity of these important, yet barely understood assets.

working definition of middle neighborhoods is that they are places that are er hot market areas with rapidly rising prices nor distressed areas with falling s and rising vacancies. Rather, these are the affordable neighborhoods in their dictions. On the edge between growth and decline, middle neighborhoods generally affordable, stable, and safe, and they historically have played an rtant role building opportunity and prosperity.

Just as rising prices from gentrification can force out long-term residents, a fai middle neighborhood can have devastating trigger effects on its residents an municipality. Whether property values skyrocket or plummet, residents are at of being forced out. Too often the heaviest toll falls on the modest-income fam and households. When neighborhoods decline, large numbers of modest-inc households, many of whom are people of color, lose wealth due to declining h price, widening the wealth gap in the nation. Failing middle neighborhoods jeopardize municipal and school budgets as well as increase appeals for fec and state support because declining home values mean a loss of property revenues. Despite their importance, middle neighborhoods are the subject of few strategic interventions and policies. Nor is there consensus among scho about what factors tip them in one direction or another.

By way of background, in August 2016, the Federal Reserve Bank of San Franc dedicated its *Community Investment Review* to the topic of middle neighborho The American Assembly then published an updated version of this conten *On the Edge: America's Middle Neighborhoods*. Edited by Paul C. Brophy, the k consists of twelve chapters by sixteen authors on the challenges and promi practices to stabilize middle neighborhoods. The book has been widely and discussed by neighborhood experts following a national rollout with ev in Detroit, New Orleans, Chicago, San Francisco, St. Louis, and Philadelp culminating in a Congressional briefing in Washington, D.C.

"We have to understand who lives in middle neighborhoods. These are neighborhoods of teachers, firefighters, and hospital workers. These residents provide our city's tax base and their neighborhoods must provide a decent quality of life for them— if not, those who can leave, will leave." —Barbara Aylesworth, Senior Program Officer, Healthy Neighborhoods, Baltimore

ıkee neighborhood association Capitol Heights hosts community event at the local school to provide residents with discounted flowers and plants. credit: Antoinette Vaughn.

The book and outreach activities were organized to:

- Help practitioners, policymakers, and advocates understand that impro
  middle neighborhoods is a distinct area of practice, research, and investm
- Build public awareness and understanding, including bipartisan supp
  around the important role middle neighborhoods play in stabili
  communities and the urban economy.
- Create long-term initiatives and partnerships to advance the fiel
  middle neighborhood improvement.

The goal of the Baltimore convening on November 15–16, 2017
to strengthen the nascent interest in stabilizing middle neighborho
Framed as an action agenda for a national movement, the convening sou
to advance thinking and action on middle neighborhoods. Among
participants were the Mayor of Baltimore, Catherine E. Pugh; Philadelphia
Council representative, Cherelle Parker; and two members of Congress, Rep.
Kildee (D-MI) and Rep. Dwight Evans (D-PA). Experts from varying discipl
and backgrounds were divided into three working groups: policy, practice,
research. All had an interest in advancing cross-sectoral solutions given
prominent role nonprofit organizations, philanthropy, and financial institut
play in determining outcomes.

This summary provides highlights of the meeting. More information is avail
at www.middleneighborhoods.org.

> "Today you can invest in a company that makes a
> pill that lowers blood pressure, but you can't invest
> in a neighborhood that does the same thing."
> —David Erickson, Director, Community
> Development Department, Federal
> Reserve Bank of San Francisco

A decisive determinant of the appropriate policies and practices for middle neighborhoods is their market context.

ıre actions to improve middle neighborhoods must be based on and
ınce practice. This approach grounded the meeting. It also ensured
each of the three issue areas (policy, practice, and research) took into
ount the key fact that targeted actions by practitioners are necessary to
ilize middle neighborhoods. While each of the working groups identified
screet set of recommendations and topics for further work (summarized
w and detailed in appendices) that link up with practice in varying ways,
e are contextual issues critical to understanding the major conclusions of
middle neighborhoods framework on which these recommendations are
d. These include:

- **MARKET CONTEXT:** A decisive determinant of the appropriate policies and
  practices for middle neighborhoods is their market context. In many
  cities and suburbs with weak housing markets (e.g. Detroit, Baltimore,

Cleveland) middle neighborhood interventions need to have
goal of preventing these neighborhoods from falling into decline
hot housing markets (e.g. San Francisco, Seattle, Washington D
policies are needed to preserve these neighborhoods for househ
with modest incomes in the face of rapidly escalating housing pri
The meeting focus was primarily on neighborhood stabilization
avoidance of decline.

- **ACCESS TO CAPITAL:** Capital for mortgages, home improveme
  housing rehabilitation, and business expansion are crucial
  middle neighborhoods. However, the private financial market is
  providing as much capital as is needed for middle neighborhoo
  This is largely because as lending institutions have consolida
  over the past thirty years, fewer banks are actively seeking custom
  in these neighborhoods due to their modest housing values—n
  banks find it less profitable to make modest-sized loans. Investme
  are also necessary for soft-asset improvements such as common ar
  and the transformation or remediation of abandoned areas i
  vibrant, open, green spaces. Yet financing for small- and large-s
  upgrading is scarce, especially in cash-strapped, weak market cit
  This dearth of capital is debilitating to many middle neighborhoo
  and remedies to this condition are essential to their stabilization c
  the short- and long-term.

- **BUILD FROM STRENGTH:** Middle neighborhoods are generally div
  by race, class, and age. They are by nature mixed, with some hav
  a mix of housing types for rent as well as home ownership. M
  importantly, given the large portion of middle class Americans li
  in them, they are crucial to the livelihood for those that are neit
  poor, nor affluent. Although it may seem counterintuitive to so
  rather than limiting recovery work to the weakest parts of a city, a
  revitalization approach is to build upon the assets—physical, soc
  and economic—found in middle neighborhoods. This "build f
  strength" approach typically has the effect of "spreading the brig
  as a strategy to "prevent the blight." Stabilizing middle neighborho
  and more distressed neighborhoods at the same time—especially w
  they are adjacent and share schools, parks, playgrounds, and ot
  amenities—creates an opportunity to extend the strength of mic
  neighborhoods into more distressed communities. In order to ca
  out this approach, participants spoke of the need to align advoca

"Many foundations have done tremendous things through heavy investment in downtowns, especially in highly distressed cities. But in order to stabilize housing markets, funders are going to have to diversify their approach and address the barriers to middle neighborhood investment."
—Alicia Kitsuse, Program Director,
The Funders Network for Smart
Growth and Livable Communities

outside of a local bakery in Chatham, a project supported by the Greater Chatham Initiative in Chicago. Photo credit: Aly Andrews.

for middle neighborhoods with advocates for the lowest inco
populations. Linking up and partnering also helps to avoid the
of "false choices" that can mislead policymakers to weigh the n
of middle-income residents against low-income constituents, or
interests of homeowners against renters.

policy focus can be captured by one question: why do local, state, and
onal policymakers ignore middle neighborhoods, despite the fact that
house almost half of urban residents and provide a substantial amount
evenue to local governments, often the primary source of funds for public
ices to residents and businesses throughout their jurisdictions? Or, to use
ealth analogy: why do we wait for neighborhoods to decline and then give
m remedial medicine—which is often expensive and/or ineffective—rather
n giving neighborhoods vitamins and nutrition to keep them healthy?

elated question is also pertinent: why are these neighborhoods important
heir cities and suburbs? Participants focused on two main reasons why
dle neighborhoods are essential to the people living in them and to their
ounding jurisdictions.

- First, these neighborhoods typically contain a substantial number
  of homeowners, and a decline in home values means that these
  homeowners will lose their home equity, reducing family wealth. Home
  equity is the most important wealth-builder among modest-income
  Americans. Increase of home equity can lead to inter-generational
  upward mobility while loss of home equity often threatens the financial
  stability of homeowners and their families.

- Second, these neighborhoods are a vital component of the property
  tax base of cities, suburbs, and school districts. Reductions in property
  values create a loss of property tax revenue to a municipality, making
  it difficult or impossible to provide high quality municipal services

and good schools. Modest and steady growth of property values provide local governments and schools with the necessary resou to improve services for businesses and residents throughout t city or suburbs. Ensuring property value growth will solidify a l jurisdiction's budget, preventing state take-over resulting from def or a precipitous revenue decline.

At the federal level, participants recommended the implementation of a lim federal pilot program in which the Federal Housing Administration, Far Mae, and Freddie Mac could assist millennials to restructure their student l debt to facilitate the purchase of previously foreclosed real estate owned (R homes. Discussion also focused on amending the Community Reinvestn Act and Internal Revenue Service regulations to encourage further investn by financial institutions and foundations into middle neighborhoods.

Three significant issues and recommendations relevant to federal policy emer

- Most federal programs aimed at improving neighborhoods focused on places where there are high concentrations of lo income people. This targeting is typically done through means-te program assistance for housing rehabilitation and other progra Adhering to strict qualifications and definitions rightly ensures the most vulnerable populations receive access to much nee funding. However, despite the acute need for middle neighborh investment and stabilization in a weak market setting, as is the case in the Healthy Neighborhoods program in Baltimore, there is no federal support available to strengthen middle neighborhoods. Federal policies that balance financial help to people in need with places in need are necessary in cities and suburbs seeking to stabilize their middle neighborhoods.

- The lingering legacy of mortgage redlining, racial disparity in real estate appraisals and valuation, absence of laws preventing discrimination against a person's source of income, and the disinvestment in transportation infrastructure and school construction also impair middle neighborhoods. Current policies are typically focused on the needs of the most blighted or economically challenged communities, Government budgeting and appropriation processes are more responsive to advocates representing specific demographic and special interest constituencies, than on diverse, mixed-income neighborhoods.

- A federal demonstration program to improve middle neighborhoods— one based on the principles and activities of existing successful pilot programs—would go a long way to testing the value and viability of middle neighborhood intervention strategies in different market settings.

vever, given the current national political climate, the group noted the
 prospect of the federal government addressing the needs of middle
hborhoods through policy tools and initiatives such as tax credits and block
ts. Instead, future policy solutions are likely to be narrow in scope and
lly based. In discussing what could be done at the local and state levels in
of federal support, the group cited the need for neighborhood revitalization
philanthropy programs that forego income restrictions and employ mixed
me strategies. Other group recommendations include capacity building
technical assistance resources to support community-based organizations,
eownership incentives, and schools—especially charter schools—that draw
llment from their surrounding neighborhoods. Adopting collaborative
els for new school construction that allow neighborhood organizations and
s from nearby middle and more distressed neighborhoods to weigh in on
school's development and future operations helps create good schools, and
ds community cohesion.

Among the guiding principles that framed the group's deliberations
conclusions was the broad definition of "policy" to encompass the initiat
of nonprofit and private entities, including financial institutions. The gr
also recommended engaging anchor institutions, such as educational
medical institutions, located in, or near, middle neighborhoods. In recogni
of the close interaction between policy and practice, the group recommen
that policies for middle neighborhoods should be based on a thoro
understanding of how successful interventions work at the grassroots le
Helping stakeholders from across the political spectrum better understand
immediate and future needs of middle neighborhoods is also critically impor
to building support for middle neighborhood policies.

> *Among the guiding principles that framed th
> (Policy) group's deliberations and conclusion
> was the broad definition of "policy" to
> encompass the initiatives of nonprofit and
> private entities, including financial institution*

The morass of red tape that hobbles improving middle neighborhoods was c
among structural policy obstacles. Unfunded mandates for sewer upgra
cumbersome tax abatement, code enforcement, and foreclosure disposi
procedures likewise hinder efforts to adequately address the challenge
property vacancies. These municipal hurdles were cited in other groups as v

A more complete list of policies benefiting middle neighborhoods is include
Appendix 1. While some of the suggestions are limited in scope and relati
simple to implement, the Policy Working Group agreed that more resea
deliberation, and framing is required to translate the ideas into actual polic
legislative actions.

ariety of neighborhood-based practitioners and local governments are
:ing successfully to stabilize middle neighborhoods. The meeting succeeded
>nnecting some of these individuals for the first time, creating a community
·actitioners who can now exchange best practices and become a collective
: for improving middle neighborhoods. Some of the practitioners are staff
ommunity development corporations (CDC), while others work with a
:ty of organizations locally, regionally, or nationally. A complete list of the
nizations that participated in the Practice Working Group is available at
·.middleneighborhoods.org.

work of middle neighborhood practitioners can be far reaching, and the
p identified their fifteen primary challenges. (These are described in
endix 2, along with approaches for how each of the topics can be addressed.)
topics range from outdated housing stock and public safety to measurement
performance indicators and job training for residents. There was significant
·ergence within the group around communications, including how to
gthen the case for why it's important to support middle neighborhoods.
cipants described the need to have clear and compelling narratives and
uage to address multiple audiences: investors who need to understand the
:et potential of investing in these neighborhoods; local policymakers (and
:times local philanthropies) who do not perceive these neighborhoods as being
;k or may be entirely focused on distressed neighborhoods; and community
bers who are more concerned about gentrification than decline, despite facts
indicate decline as the more important threat. Low internal capacity was
identified as an important issue among the organizations represented at the
:ing. Many described the challenge of executing strategic programs while

providing basic neighborhood and community development services by alre
understaffed organizations.

In identifying barriers, the practitioners discussed the same unfair and outd
lending practices identified by the policy group. The practitioners also foc
on potential new approaches to the sale of real estate. Of primary concern is
failure of the commission-based system to provide incentives that address
needs of middle neighborhood homes given their generally low to modest pric

Practitioners utilize a combination of approaches to improve mi
neighborhoods: mutual neighborhood self-help; collaboration with len
making market-rate loans to improve properties; marketing these of
overlooked areas; and various forms of local government support. The majc
of approaches outlined were characterized as work that could be advance
practitioners, such as developing effective community engagement strate
aimed at organizing residents into informal and formal associations.

ust work is underway across the nation by organizations that recognize unique position of middle neighborhoods as places on the edge. These nizations have broadened the typical range of community development ices, offering services and resources that help to stabilize neighborhoods for ent and future residents. A summary of the services and resources these nizations provide appears in the middle neighborhood organization grid on following pages.

neighborhoods these organizations serve are identified below.

- Greater Milwaukee Foundation: Capitol Heights and 12 others
- Capitol Heights: Capitol Heights
- Greater Chatham Initiative: Chatham, Greater Grand Crossing, Avalon Park, Auburn Gresham
- Old Brooklyn Community Development Corporation: Old Brooklyn
- Slavic Village Development: Slavic Village
- The City of Geneva: Hildreth Hill and 10 others
- NeighborWorks Rochester: Triangle, Swillburg, Brooks Landing, Pocket
- Healthy Neighborhoods Inc.: Belair-Edison, Waverly and 40 others
- Strong City Baltimore: Waverly and 9 others
- Jubilee Baltimore: Midtown, Central City, Southeast Baltimore
- Belair-Edison Neighborhoods, Inc.: Belair-Edison
- Mt. Airy USA: Mount Airy
- The City of Philadelphia: (Applications pending)

	ORGANIZATION	GREATER MILWAUKEE FOUNDATION	CAPITOL HEIGHTS	GREATER CHATHAM INITIATIVE	OLD BROOKLYN CDC	SLAVIC DEVELO…
	CITY	MILWAUKEE, WI	MILWAUKEE, WI	CHICAGO, IL	CLEVELAND, OH	CLEVEL…
	NEIGHBORHOODS SERVED	13	1	4	1	
SOURCES OF FUNDING	EARNED REVENUE			✔	✔	✔
	PRIVATE LENDERS					
	FOUNDATIONS	✔	✔	✔	✔	✔
	CITY		✔	✔	✔	
	STATE		✔			
	FEDERAL		✔		✔	✔
DIRECT SERVICES	BUY, REHAB, & SELL HOMES			✔	✔	✔
	COMMUNITY ORGANIZING	✔	✔	✔	✔	✔
	BUSINESS DEVELOPMENT			✔	✔	✔
	CODE ENFORCEMENT				✔	
	HOMEOWNERSHIP COUNSELING	✔		✔		
	RESIDENT TRAINING	✔				
	FORECLOSURE PREVENTION	✔		✔		
	VACANT PROPERTY MANAGEMENT					
	FACILITATE HISTORIC TAX CREDITS					
ACCESS TO CAPITAL	HOME EQUITY/IMPROVEMENT LOANS		✔	✔	✔	✔
	FHA REHAB LOANS			✔		
	MATCHING GRANTS	✔		✔		
	DEVELOP & MANAGE LOAN PROGRAM					
MARKETING	MARKETING STRATEGY	✔		✔	✔	✔
	WEB & SOCIAL MEDIA OUTREACH	✔	✔	✔	✔	✔
	VISUAL IDENTITY & SIGNAGE	✔		✔	✔	✔
OTHER INITIATIVES	EXTERIOR IMPROVEMENTS	✔		✔	✔	
	PUBLIC ART & CULTURAL PROGRAMMING	✔			✔	✔
	YOUTH, FAMILY, & EDUCATION	✔	✔	✔	✔	✔
	SAFETY	✔	✔	✔	✔	✔
	WORKFORCE & TRANSPORTATION	✔	✔	✔		
	HEALTH & FOOD	✔			✔	✔

GENEVA	NEIGHBORWORKS ROCHESTER	HEALTHY NEIGHBORHOODS	STRONG CITY BALTIMORE	JUBILEE BALTIMORE	BELAIR-EDISON NEIGHBORHOODS	MT. AIRY USA	CITY OF PHILADELPHIA
VA, NY	ROCHESTER, NY	BALTIMORE, MD	BALTIMORE, MD	BALTIMORE, MD	BALTIMORE, MD	PHILA., PA	PHILA., PA
1	4	42	10	3	1	1	43
		✓	✓	✓		✓	
							✓
✓	✓	✓	✓	✓	✓	✓	✓
✓		✓				✓	✓
✓		✓	✓	✓	✓	✓	✓
✓	✓	✓	✓	✓	✓	✓	✓
		✓	✓	✓		✓	✓
✓	✓		✓	✓	✓		✓
	✓		✓		✓	✓	✓
✓	✓		✓		✓		✓
	✓			✓	✓	✓	✓
✓		✓		✓	✓	✓	✓
	✓	✓			✓	✓	✓
			✓				✓
				✓			
	✓	✓	✓	✓	✓		✓
✓		✓	✓	✓	✓		
✓		✓		✓	✓		✓
		✓					✓
✓	✓	✓	✓	✓	✓		
✓	✓	✓	✓	✓	✓	✓	
✓	✓	✓			✓	✓	✓
✓	✓	✓	✓		✓	✓	✓
	✓	✓	✓		✓		✓
		✓	✓		✓	✓	✓
✓		✓	✓		✓	✓	✓
					✓		✓
	✓				✓		✓

In an effort to illustrate the impact of these organizations, below are profiles of middle neighborhood stabilization efforts in five cities. Three (Baltimore, Cleveland, and Rochester) operate in cities where overall weak market conditions influence the availability of resources and political will to implement neighborhood revitalization strategies. More competitive real estate markets in Chicago and Philadelphia present a different set of challenges and opportunities for middle neighborhood practitioners.

Before: 2200 block of Callow Avenue in Reservoir Hill, Bal
Photo credit: Healthy Neighborhoods, Inc.

BALTIMORE

For over fifteen years, the Healthy Neighborhoods, Inc. (HNI) program in Baltimore has been successfully working with neighborhood residents, government, lending institutions, and others to stabilize and improve forty-neighborhoods. In most of the middle neighborhoods involved in the progr housing prices are trending upward, and vacant houses, when they occur, being rehabilitated and sold. A majority of the funding is made possible pooled private loan fund that has attracted thirteen lenders active in the One of the advantages of private financing is that it does not place restricti on applicants' incomes. Middle neighborhoods working with HNI have provi $70 million for existing and new homeowners to buy, refinance, and reno homes. This included $26 million in federal Neighborhood Stabilization Prog funds, made available through the American Recovery and Reinvestment A that limited eligibility to borrowers earning up to 120% area median inco (AMI). Another $30 million private fund scheduled for launch in 2018 forego income restrictions. A matching grant program made possible thro allocations of city revenues places modest income restrictions on eligibility. Th grants provide up to $10,000 for home rehabilitation. In addition, HNI prov funds to community-based organizations for marketing efforts and reside driven neighborhood improvement projects such as commissioning public ar supporting other "curb appeal" or exterior improvements. For example, the Be Edison CDC, located in a northeast African-American Baltimore neighborh with a median household income of $46,700, has been working for over a dec

rengthen housing prices and build community fabric. It has directly helped
ty-six homeowners buy and/or improve their homes through loans worth
3 million, facilitated eighty-six additional resident-led block projects, and
vated 200 large and small commercial building improvement projects worth
e than $5.5 million. Housing prices have risen in Belair-Edison building home
ty, yet the median home price in 2017 was a modest $60,000.

ELAND

eland Neighborhood Progress, a citywide community development funding
mediary, is working to stabilize a number of city and suburban middle
hborhoods. Like many other legacy cities, Cleveland has suffered over fifty years
opulation decline following the loss of the manufacturing and other industries,
rn creating a number of socioeconomic problems. Over the past thirty years,
h attention has been paid to neighborhoods with concentrated poverty in these
s. Now, focus is also building around middle neighborhoods. For example, the
Brooklyn CDC is improving Old Brooklyn, a middle neighborhood located on
dge of the city. Old Brooklyn is Cleveland's largest neighborhood, with 35,000
ents. After identifying the trend of declining income levels, the CDC's first
was to correct the misperception that its middle-class base is stable. In 2015,
en adopted a middle neighborhood strategy focused on community health and
eting programs, in addition to buying, rehabilitating, and selling single-family

Residents of Old Brooklyn at the annual Pedal for Prizes event, which encourages participants to explore the Cleveland neighborhood by
Photo credit: Old Brooklyn Community Development Corporation.

homes. Its programs include organizing block clubs, crime watch, family and yo
events, and utilizing social media to brand the neighborhood. Like many o
middle neighborhoods, Old Brooklyn's challenges are becoming more sever
household wealth declines and funding resources are increasingly scarce.

ROCHESTER

Rochester's city government is evaluating the possibility of expanding on
success of NeighborWorks Rochester's Healthy Blocks initiative. Since 2005,
program has stabilized three middle neighborhoods, and is now working wit
fourth, the Triangle neighborhood. Selection criteria for Healthy Blocks inc
the prevalence of increasing poverty concentrations. Positive outcomes have l
greatest in neighborhoods that are wedged between a stronger neighborhoo
one side and a more distressed one on the other. Critical to the initiative's suc
has been a core group of active residents' and merchants' associations that l
worked together to plan and implement social events, public space improven
projects, property improvement promotion efforts, and neighborhood marke
strategies. Practitioners from Rochester described the positive impact within
communities of clarifying the goals of its work—stabilization, not gentrifica
Healthy Blocks has made substantial progress in helping officials in
government understand the importance of stabilizing middle neighborhoods.

"In Rochester, our mayor and city council members have been conceptually supportive of a middle neighborhoods focus but are concerned about trade-offs with more distressed areas, so we have reframed the conversation to one about comprehensive planning to look at intervention alternatives for all neighborhood types, including our middle neighborhoods."
—Dorraine Kirkmire, Manager of Planning, City of Rochester

YOU
change
GROWTH
WE
together
FAMILI

…eted mural in the Triangle neighborhood, Rochester. Photo credit: Mikey Vargas-Rodriguez.

Street banners and signs are part of the branding efforts by the Greater Chatham Initiative in Chicago. Photo credit: Greater Chatham Initi

Greater Chatham Initiative in Chicago is a comprehensive effort to improve
ng-standing middle income African-American Southside neighborhood.
ncludes strategies to improve housing as well as fostering economic
lopment, job growth, and employment recruitment. In 2016, the Greater
tham neighborhood began implementing a strategic plan that aligns four
nct neighborhoods as a single community, allowing them to compete more
essively among the seventy-seven neighborhoods that make up the city of
ago. The Greater Chatham marketing strategy includes creating a single
t of engagement website that showcases a specific neighborhood brand
tity that targets younger audiences. Over 150 retail and business-to-business
s for local stakeholders are identified on the site's neighborhood map. Part of
way Greater Chatham measures success is by unemployment and economic
lopment indicators that measure targeted support and outcomes for firms—
 those that are located in the neighborhood and firms in other areas of the
where neighborhood residents work. Outcomes include increased revenues
firms in metal fabrication, transportation, distribution and logistics, and
 processing and packaging. Over 150 residents are engaged in six working
mittees and many more through volunteer activities.

ADELPHIA

hiladelphia, local policy measures to stabilize middle neighborhoods have
 underway since 2008 when the City launched an extensive foreclosure
ention program at the height of the subprime mortgage crisis. Later, when
lopment pressure intensified, they adopted a tax relief program to prevent
displacement of long-time homeowners. Still, middle neighborhoods lack the
s the need to attract sufficient interest from the private sector. Philadelphia
w in the process of launching a program that offers low-interest loans to
eowners who need assistance but are above the income threshold for free
e repair. Less restrictive income eligibility can allow for more targeted support
ouseholds and neighborhoods at risk of decline. Leading public discourse in
adelphia on the importance of stabilizing middle neighborhoods are advocates
City Council President Darrell Clarke and Councilwoman Cherelle Parker,
 represent districts where new strategies are needed to protect working class
hborhoods.

A number of inferences about successful practice can be made from mid
neighborhood stabilization efforts in these five cities:

1. Organized, grassroots neighborhood residents are the key players
    stabilizing middle neighborhoods. These groups are often supported
    local foundations and/or a citywide organization tasked with the goa
    improving these areas. Healthy Neighborhoods, Inc. in Baltimore
    leading illustration of this kind of organization. Government rarely p
    more than a supportive role in the improvement of middle neighborho

2. The goals of those working to prevent middle neighborhoods dec
    are to stabilize and increase property values, thereby making
    neighborhood a good investment for homeowners and other prop
    owners—in other words, to create a well-functioning housing marke

3. The approaches to improvement typically involve organizing neighb
    to work together to build from neighborhood assets, make improveme
    and fight off threats to neighborhood stability. Most programs comb
    modest physical improvements to common space, exterior renovat
    to homes, crime reduction efforts, enhancements to school quality,
    neighborhood marketing. These efforts help signal market segments
    the neighborhood may, in fact, be a housing bargain.

4. More capital is crucial to the well-being of middle neighborhoods
    some instances, banks have committed to increasing lending for h
    purchase and improvements, but this element is not widespread
    some cities, Community Development Financial Institutions (CD
    are playing a key role in providing capital.

ough chapters in *On the Edge* describe some of the characteristics and market
litions of middle neighborhoods, much more research is needed. In order to
ess this need, the researchers who attended the meeting developed a research
da that will deepen the nation's collective understanding of the dynamics
trajectories of middle neighborhoods: where these neighborhoods are, who
 in them, and what factors drive their trajectories.

n the focus on the practice of stabilizing middle neighborhoods, the group
ed future research should identify the forces that lead middle neighborhoods
it tipping points into decline or gentrification, and what can be done to
ent these tipping points from being reached. The primary research questions
ide: which middle neighborhoods are threatened with decline? Which are
y to be affected by escalating prices, moving them from affordable to modest-
me households to accessible only for households with higher-incomes? The
p concluded that this examination must include suburban areas as well as
ral city neighborhoods as many older suburbs are also encountering the perils
cline or gentrification.

s agreed that this research must be conducted both from a historic perspective
with a future lens. Future threats to middle neighborhoods include climate
ge, changes in national policies, economic dislocation, and social instability.
ldition, the group called for research to track the effectiveness of middle
hborhoods improvement programs. (See Appendix 3 for the detailed report
 the research group. The Lincoln Institute of Land Policy is leading part of
nitial research in partnership with the Center for Community Progress.)

The Research Working Group agreed on a path of action in three areas:

DOCUMENTING THE POLICY PROBLEM

- Define middle neighborhoods and document their prevalence location in a sample of American cities with different market contexts.
- Document trends in middle neighborhoods. Have they shrunk in recent decades? In which cities have middle neighborhoods fared the best the worst?
- Develop a typology of middle neighborhoods.
  - Strong versus weak market metropolitan areas.
  - Middle neighborhoods threatened by decline versus those threatened by gentrification.
  - Downtown core and central city versus suburban.
- Develop an understanding about benefits of middle neighborhoods what will be lost if they disappear.
- Examine future opportunities and threats to middle neighborhoods.
- Develop an understanding about benefits of middle neighborhoods what might be lost, if they disappear.
  - To individuals: how do middle neighborhoods contribute to mobility and opportunity for residents?
  - To cities and regions: how are middle neighborhoods important the fiscal health of cities, suburbs, and regions?

orhood association Capitol Heights runs a summer youth work program in Milwaukee. Photo credit: Antoinette Vaughn.

ERSTANDING THE TRAJECTORIES OF MIDDLE NEIGHBORHOODS

- Quantitative research: what are the trends in middle neighborhoods and what factors and characteristics are associated with both stability and instability?
- Qualitative research: what can be learned from case studies of successful and unsuccessful middle neighborhoods? What are the threats to middle neighborhoods? What are the opportunities for successful interventions?

EMINATING THE RESEARCH

- Distill the research findings into reports that can be helpful to practitioners and policymakers.

"It's on us to build and strengthen our middle neighborhoods because this is a real opportunity for us to make things happen. And given how unlikely it is that we'll find help from our federal government, we have to seize every opportunity we can find to help one another and raise the consciousness."
—Congressman Dwight Evans

conclusion, the meeting succeeded in strengthening a core group of essionals, elected officials, and neighborhood leaders committed to stabilizing lle neighborhoods. Participants agreed that a national movement—based he remarkable work of practitioners, residents, and local governments—is essary and urgent. While many questions about the focus of the movement till unresolved, the rationale for action is clear: the price of neglect is far too icious and costly.

can be seen in many cities, middle neighborhoods provide a lifeline—for eowners as well as renters—to the American middle class. They are the places re equitable economic mobility occurs, and where community organizing, tive public service, good schools, and private sector growth all coalesce. iring their stability while preserving their diversity is crucially important. A step is to create a bipartisan, national coalition for middle neighborhoods. coalition must bring together elected and appointed officials, civic and anthropic leaders, and neighborhood practitioners to advance policies and tices to improve middle neighborhoods at the local, state, and federal levels.

IERSHIP

ling from the work of participants at the Baltimore meeting, a number of middle hborhood practitioners and institutional partners have been engaged to identify re middle neighborhood initiatives. The organizations involved include: The erican Assembly, Lincoln Institute of Land Policy, The Local Initiatives Support ooration (LISC), National Alliance of Community Economic Development ociations (NACEDA), the National Urban League, NeighborWorks America, the Urban Institute, among other Regional Federal Reserve Banks.

An important issue to address with regards to leadership is determining how policy, practice, and research strands will be integrated. While the meeting divided into these tracts for detailed discussion, aligning action across the th areas will be necessary to improve middle neighborhoods and sustain the emerg national movement. As of February 2018, the Lincoln Institute of Land Po has committed to conducting initial research focused on middle neighborho through collaboration with the Center for Community Progress. The Ameri Assembly continues to administer an ongoing working group of practitioners Community of Practice) on an interim basis. Additional organizations need to identified to lead practice and policy, and to serve as the overall integrator coordinator over the long-term.

NECESSARY ACTION COMPONENTS

Each of the three working groups identified important issues, desi resources, and next steps specific to their group's needs. While the cumula lists are extensive, there is substantive overlap among these need particularly with regard to data-rich evidence on middle neighborh characteristics and trajectories to illuminate when and how to interve Most participants agreed that future work should aim to equip commu development practitioners, lenders, and policymakers with practical resou for stabilizing middle neighborhoods.

The following resources would address these collective needs. While prima tailored to those already engaged in middle neighborhood stabilization, th resources would also be instructive for those new to the field.

GUIDEBOOK. A guidebook including typologies and defining characteristic middle neighborhoods in various market contexts, supported by illustra examples in cities and suburbs, and potentially rural areas was recommen Typologies should include various trajectories for middle neighborhoods in t regional market context, assessing risk factors of decline and gentrificat primary demographic and socio-economic trends, regulatory challenges, po issues, and forward-looking threats such as climate change. This informa would be presented through easy-to-follow text and images.

The Guidebook would also include:

- Detailed case studies and best practices of successful market stabiliza
  strategies: how each strategy works; policies and programs th
  strategies utilize; sources of financing, roles and responsibilities of

"Middle neighborhood residents represent
50+% of their city's population. If
they mobilized as a constituency, then
there would be more political power to
do neighborhood revitalization."
—Joe McNeely, President,
Metroscape Development

organizations; and indicators and outcomes in target neighborhoods as well as those in distressed adjacent areas. These assessments would include changes in home values, income levels, racial equity, occupancy, crime, local economic development, and school performance.

- A practical narrative detailing how organizations leading middle neighborhood improvement work have determined where and how to invest, as well as lessons learned, and course corrections adopted toward stabilization.

EY. A state-by-state or city-by-city compilation of organizations driving le neighborhoods work across the nation is needed. The survey would identify nizations conducting stabilization efforts, including how each organization es its program's terms, constituency, approaches, available resources, market reach. The survey would be administered by an organization with nal reach. An important task at the outset will be defining the methods for cting, aggregating, and publishing responses to ensure they are in easy-to-use accessible, interactive formats. The survey would also include information t available middle neighborhood resources (e.g. available financing for ades, technical assistance, etc.) for each state or city. These resources would

"Since starting the Healthy Neighborhoods program in 2000, we've been able to strengthen ties between neighborhood residents, increase home values, and encourage millions of dollars of investment into communities here in Baltimore—and I'm excited about the possibility for communities across the country to do this as well."
—Johnette Richardson, Executive Director, Belair-Edison Neighborhoods Inc.

ompiled nationally and distributed alongside the national results; they can be tailored for distribution to individual cities and states.

ddition to the Guidebook and Survey, the following resources and activities e identified by the Practice Working Group to both strengthen the work of titioners and recruit others interested in adopting middle neighborhood tegies in their areas.

MUNITY OF PRACTICE. The newly-formed Community of Practice has subdivided committees organized around specialized topics, such as identifying and gorizing the various middle neighborhood typologies, identifying best tices, recruiting and onboarding new members, and conducting outreach. h the requisite organizational and institutional support, this group has the ntial to scale its efforts nationally.

KITS. Given the Practice Working Group's emphasis on organizational capacity ding, toolkits were identified as a priority resource. While not exhaustive, the wing list would help equip community leaders and partners with important rmation about how to strengthen and stabilize middle neighborhoods:

- How to develop a loan program.
- How to create greater racial equity in middle neighborhoods.
- How to market the neighborhood to attract new and diverse residents.
- How to adopt new strategies for engaging existing residents in neighborhood stabilization efforts.

TRAINING. Given the emphasis on capacity building, training is a necessary foll
on activity. Training sessions would target practitioners to facilitate peer-to-
knowledge exchange and mentorship around issues such as achieving r
equity, adopting asset-based approaches to revitalization, workforce developm
resident engagement for public safety measures, and marketing tactics an
others. Documenting and recording training sessions for online posting ena
unlimited access these resources. These online resources would also e
practitioners and policymakers with the necessary communication and teac
tools for redistribution to their constituents and partners. Policymaker trai
would address issues such as:

- How to support practitioners.
- How to coordinate investment and community revitalization an
  middle neighborhoods and more distressed communities simultaneo
- How to align and increase access to capital in middle neighborhood
- How to make tough decisions about which neighborhoods to target.
- What are mechanisms to spur investment in both hard and soft asse

SITE VISITS. Seeing first hand evidence of the success of the Hea
Neighborhoods, Inc. program in Baltimore prompted practitioners to cal
greater investment in peer-to-peer exchange through site visits to cities
established middle neighborhood programs.

CONVENING. A larger follow-up national meeting involving a more diverse g
of practitioners, funders, and lenders was recommended. The meeting woul
organized around the exchange of best practices and training.

r Dolkart
onal Community Development Manager
ral Reserve Bank of Richmond

Policy Working Group was primarily charged with the assignment of
tifying and evaluating the federal and local policies that affect Middle
ghborhoods. The participants recommended potential changes to existing
ral and local laws and regulations and formulated new initiatives that could
igthen these communities. These discussions were facilitated by co-chairs
relle Parker, a member of the Philadelphia City Council, and Joe McNeely,
teran community development consultant and founding director of the
tral Baltimore Partnership. The Group's membership included federal and
l elected officials and their staff; a City Housing Commissioner; a State
stant Secretary for Neighborhood Revitalization; city planners, economic
lopment practitioners, researchers, and advocates; and senior community
lopment staff from the Federal Reserve Banks of Philadelphia, Richmond,
San Francisco.

n the opening deliberations, the contributors' diverse backgrounds in practice
policy distinctly influenced the direction of the discussions and conclusions
the course of the day. The group quickly adopted a broader definition of
icy" beyond government programs to incorporate the initiatives of private and
profit players as well as anchor and financial institutions. The participants
ed that the boundary between policy and practice is virtually indiscernible
therefore any formulation of policy affecting middle neighborhoods should be
sed on solving practical problems. They resolved to avoid the fallacy of "false
ces" that could mislead policymakers to weigh the interests of homeowners
ist renters and low-income constituents against middle-income residents.
lly, the group recognized that the current national political climate made
iously reliable policy initiatives such as tax credits, block grants, transportation

infrastructure, and school construction unpredictable and therefore future po
solutions are likely to be narrow in scope, locally based, and initially focused
changing public perceptions of middle neighborhoods.

The Policy Working Group listed and evaluated both traditional and innova
financing, housing, and education policies and then determined if these progr
were positively impacting "on-the-edge neighborhoods." The participa
identified several supportive neighborhood revitalization and philanthr
initiatives that strengthen middle neighborhoods, because they were not inco
restricted and employed mixed income and regional, place-based strateg
This list included examples of housing programs in Philadelphia, where (
of households are eligible to benefit from home ownership counseling
foreclosure mitigation assistance. In Maryland, both the *Healthy Neighborho*
and the *Baltimore Regional Neighborhoods Initiative* were highlighted as model
both nonprofit and government initiated programs that promote homeowner
and provide technical assistance to community based organizations in m
income neighborhoods. The group also identified charter school policies
purposely draw their enrollment from their immediate surrounding communi
and school construction design projects that collaborate with the adjac
neighborhood associations and parent teacher associations.

Conversely, the Policy Working Group also identified examples of progr
and historic practices that, due to racial bias and structural restrictions, v
impairing middle neighborhood stabilization. The lingering legacy of mortg
redlining, racial disparity in real estate appraisals and valuation, the abse
of laws preventing discrimination against a person's source of income, and
disinvestment in transportation infrastructure and school construction v
raised. Participants also listed current policies that were too narrowly focused
on the needs of the most blighted or economically challenged communities
government budgeting and appropriation processes that were more responsiv
advocates representing specific demographic and special interest constituen
rather than diverse and mixed income neighborhoods. Additional struct
policy obstacles the group cited included unfunded mandates for sewer upgra
and cumbersome tax abatement, code enforcement, and foreclosure disposi
procedures that hindered middle neighborhoods from adequately addres
property vacancies. Finally, several participants raised the lack of broadb
access in many communities as an obstacle to attracting younger residents
new businesses.

Policy Working Group catalogued policies supportive and detrimental to
lle neighborhoods on large post-it notes, and soon the meeting room's walls
covered with a lively collage of ideas. Co-chairs Parker and McNeely then
led the participants into three- and four-person subgroups. Each subgroup
ted among the listed items a policy issue that they viewed both as a priority
for which they could formulate a practical solution or initiative. Two of
four groups identified the need to provide capacity building and technical
irces to community and neighborhood organizations. They proposed a
dation-led or government funded program that could provide professional
and organize broader support coalitions to provide these organizations with
egic planning, advocacy training, and grant writing resources. This funding
d be tied to performance metrics to gauge effectiveness. A third subgroup
osed expanded local property tax credits and federal income tax credits
icentivize the purchase of a home in a middle neighborhood, with local
rnments controlling and regularly readjusting eligibility.

fourth subgroup recommended implementing a limited federal pilot program
hich the Federal Housing Administration, Fannie Mae, and Freddie Mac
d assist millennials with restructuring their student loan debt to facilitate the
hase of previously foreclosed homes. Further discussion focused on amending
Community Reinvestment Act and Internal Revenue Service regulations to
urage further grants from financial institutions, philanthropy and foundations
middle neighborhoods. However, as expressed at the onset of the discussions,
ctations were low that the current national fiscal and political climate would
ort any program other than a "demonstration project" in a single or select
congressional districts.

full Policy Working Group concluded their deliberations by agreeing that
mmediate objective of future policy should be redefining how stakeholders
across the political spectrum perceive middle neighborhoods. This includes
creation of a national movement that seeks bipartisan support; possibly
nding and adopting new vocabulary to describe these communities, and
ing a narrative of successful, sustainable community life.

Top: Philadelphia CDC Mt. Airy USA sell "Go Mt. Airy" t-shirts at an event. Bottom: Mt. Airy hosts moonlight movies and other community Photo credit: Brad Maule.

PENDIX 2: PRACTICE WORKING GROUP HIGHLIGHTS

hanie Sung
uty Director of Urban Policy
American Assembly

 objectives of the Practice Working Group were to define the training and
ning needs of practitioners working to support middle neighborhoods and
d momentum for an ongoing community of practice. The meeting was co-
ired by Nedra Sims Fears, Executive Director of the Greater Chatham
ative in Chicago, and Marcia Nedland, a community development consultant
 specializes in marketing strategies for places in the process of revitalization.
 meeting agenda was developed collaboratively by the co-chairs and meeting
icipants, a process facilitated by The American Assembly months prior to the
ting in Baltimore. Of the nineteen participants, ten are from community-
d organizations, four are nonprofit consultants working at the national level,
 represent foundations or private lenders, and one works in the public sector.
 meeting presented the first opportunity for this group to meet and engage
 peers who share the challenges of stabilizing middle neighborhoods. Based
rior conversations, there was shared understanding that if there continued
e sufficient interest and energy among the participants, the group will form
ngoing community of practice. To that end, the agenda and discussions were
ctured to define the most important issue areas for middle neighborhood
titioners, identify approaches to each issue area, and develop the necessary
cture to support an ongoing community of practice.

titioners in middle neighborhoods come from varying types of community-
d organizations that provide a wide range of services to support residents,
uding financial counseling, grant-making for small improvement projects,
h and public safety programs, and marketing training. In order to create some
nition around the practice of middle neighborhoods, the co-chairs facilitated
d discussions with participants about their work, the challenges they face,

and possible solutions. Fifteen issue areas and approaches identified by
Practice Working Group are described below.

COMMUNICATIONS. Making the case for middle neighborhoods in market, polit
and community contexts, is critical but complicated work. The lack of rele
messaging, graphics, case studies, and other communications tools has b
a barrier to connecting with key partners, including potential funders
developers, government representatives, and peers from other neighborh
organizations. Participants cited that affordable housing advocates and lea
of neighborhoods experiencing severe decline are frequently left out of mi
neighborhood strategies. Rather than competing with these neighborho
participants described the benefits of conducting middle neighborh
stabilization in alignment with anti-poverty work, especially in weak market ci

DEFINITIONS AND MEASUREMENT. Given that "middle neighborhoods" is no
commonly used term, nor a widely understood concept, participants expre
the need to adopt common criteria for defining weak, middle, and stable hou
markets. Practitioners agreed that collaborating with the research communit
a definitional framing of the middle neighborhood term would benefit their v
and help substantiate the needs of the middle neighborhood residents. Discus
centered on whether researchers or the practitioners themselves should lead
work. Additionally, tools to identify the costs and benefits of implementing mi
neighborhood strategies and methods to evaluate the impact of these strate
would be valuable for practitioners.

DEMOGRAPHIC AND ECONOMIC CHANGES. The participants catalogued a numbe
national socioeconomic trends that have negatively impacted household we
in middle neighborhoods, including increased income disparity, stagnant wa
and poor intergenerational mobility. Developing a neighborhood loan pool
help build and keep wealth in middle income households.

OBSOLETE HOUSING STOCK. Housing stock in middle neighborhoods tends to
older and outdated, creating a mismatch of available housing to the prefere
of potential home buyers or renters, especially millennials. Participants ident
financial tools that would enable community development groups to meet
demand, including higher loan to value ratio for developers and small grant
home improvements.

ORGANIZATIONAL CAPACITY. Nonprofits and local government agencies often
the capacity to implement successful middle neighborhood strategies, w

require the substantial effort of building and sustaining relationships across
tiple city-wide partners. There is usually not enough staff to design and
ement both the strategy and essential programmatic work. Participants
tified the knowledge exchange of a national community of practice as a
ible approach to building internal capacity of their organizations.

STOR AND LANDLORD PRACTICES. A number of predatory real estate practices
discussed by participants. Recommendations included policy and regulatory
ges to curb investor and landlord behavior. Some participants noted that
enforcement has in some cases become a reactive function of the police,
ributing to poor housing standards in middle neighborhoods.

NCING. The lack of available financing for homeowners is a major barrier for
lle neighborhood stabilization. Loan products for home repair or rehabilitation
ld help residents stay in their homes, as would increased public investment.

OLS. Local schools are a critical partner in planning for long term viability
iddle neighborhoods. Participants recognized the need to focus on building
ortive partnerships with neighborhood schools although many organizations
the requisite funding and staff to initiate these programs, especially given
r priorities.

TY. Middle neighborhoods must deliver on quality of life issues like crime and
ic safety of streets and parks. Participants agreed that this quality of life issue
sely linked with community engagement; one successful approach mentioned
ganizing events that bring residents together in a positive or celebratory way,
not merely as a response to crime-related activity in the neighborhood.

ST ATTITUDES. There is a clear need to address the general resistance of realtors
potential residents to predominantly black neighborhoods. Participants
mmended adopting racial equity goals as a community of practice and
iding racial equity training to neighborhood leaders.

MUNITY LEADERSHIP AND CAPACITY BUILDING. Participants identified the need to
t new methods for community organizing in order to engage the younger
ration of current residents. Connecting neighborhood-level issues to larger
y issues was identified as a way to empower new leadership. Offering
force development opportunities is an important part of community
ership and capacity building.

MARKETING/IMAGE. Practitioners need access to up-to-date marketing t[...] and trends to help them rebrand their neighborhoods and rethink assets [...] historic buildings. Sharing marketing best practices, especially between sim[...] neighborhood types in similar cities, was identified as an important functio[...] the community of practice.

PHYSICAL CONDITIONS/CURB APPEAL. Clean and attractive yards, streets, [...] sidewalks (a.k.a. "curb appeal") are an important part of making mi[...] neighborhoods attractive to newcomers. Connecting residents to resources[...] curb appeal projects could help support a culture shift towards more phys[...] maintenance of middle neighborhoods.

RETAIL. Participants identified proximity to vibrant retail districts a[...] valuable neighborhood amenity valued by potential middle neighborh[...] newcomers. Providing retail leasing subsidies could help incenti[...] commercial development.

WORKFORCE DEVELOPMENT AND JOB OPPORTUNITIES. Middle neighborhoods stru[...] to compete with downtown centers or other areas that have closer proxi[...] to work centers and/or transit systems. More training opportunities in or n[...] middle neighborhoods should be provided to residents (e.g. in home re[...] and construction) of middle neighborhoods. Another priority is workf[...] development strategies that connect youth (16-24 years old) to jobs.

GOING FORWARD

Participants generated a number of ideas for approaching each of the fifteen i[...] areas above. In an exercise to organize the list of possible approaches, particip[...] voted to determine the following as priorities: 1) Develop a middle neighborh[...] loan program, 2) Develop new engagement strategies for residents, 3) Ado[...] racial equity framework for measuring success, 4) Create language and toolki[...] engage with and avoid alienating distressed neighborhoods, and 5) Partner [...] schools. The majority of these approaches were identified as work that coul[...] accomplished by practitioners themselves.

To that end, the group validated the working assumption that an ong[...] Community of Practice would be highly valuable, and settled on a numbe[...] priority activities. They agreed on the importance of sharing best practices, [...] virtually and by holding in-person convenings of practitioners, foundati[...] and private sector lenders—similar to the Baltimore meeting. Peer-to-peer [...] visits and mentorship were among the other ideas for knowledge exchange

nimum, this Community of Practice should include those working directly
nprove middle neighborhoods. Realtors, investors, and affordable housing
titioners were also identified as potential members to enlist, to help enrich
expand the Community of Practice.

ning from successful interventions already taking place was also seen as
ly instructive for the Community of Practice. Participants expressed interest
eveloping a training curriculum and discussed the merits of providing
fication. Collecting and packaging information for toolkits came up in several
exts. A toolkit for practitioners would include marketing practices,
ics for success, and a communications framework. Some participants
called for a toolkit for investors and real estate agents that highlights
value and opportunity of middle neighborhoods. The group agreed that
rating case studies or profiles of different middle neighborhoods would be
able fundraising and marketing tools.

lly, the practitioners coalesced around the importance of advocating
ctively for the necessary policy changes identified throughout the course
ie day. This might be achieved through a national campaign to raise
eness around middle neighborhood issues. Over the course of the session,
need to establish a clear definition of middle neighborhoods became a
rring point. While all agreed that middle neighborhoods defy a uniform
size-fits-all categorization, the group expressed the practical significance
nderstanding the various features and trajectories that characterize the
e of middle neighborhoods.

APPENDIX 3: RESEARCH WORKING GROUP HIGHLIGHTS

Jessie Grogan
Urban Development Program Manager
Lincoln Institute of Land Policy

The goal of the discussion was to establish a prioritized list of research questions and approaches about middle neighborhoods for both policymakers and practitioners.

DEFINITIONAL ISSUES

The first order of business involved establishing a way of defining middle neighborhoods. The group saw value in two approaches: (1) demographics, which involves examining the movement of households in and out of neighborhoods that were once the home to working class/working income households to determine what has happened to these neighborhoods; and (2) neighborhood market dynamics, that focuses on the market position of neighborhoods in their jurisdictions and metro areas today and over time, using housing prices relative to other areas as a key measure.

Regardless of the definitional approach, the group generally agreed that the underlying importance of research on middle neighborhoods is protecting middle neighborhoods at risk of decline (which was seen as a larger concern than protecting middle neighborhoods from gentrification). The group placed more importance on understanding and predicting future change in middle neighborhoods—particularly given the interest of millennials in city life—rather than only examining historic trends. Historic analysis that identifies middle neighborhoods' tipping points can have great relevance in understanding current and future trends. Understanding these current and future trends means placing middle neighborhoods in their regional contexts, as the aggregate number of housing units relative to population changes has big potential effects on demand for middle neighborhoods.

se broad regional housing supply issues also need to be researched in the
text of housing demand categories, such as the market for starter homes in
le neighborhoods, long-term resident communities, and neighborhoods
: appear to be middle—but may be statistically transitioning from high to
incomes or from low to high incomes. These market categories need to
understood in terms of the broad economic trends that are shrinking the
dle class.

Research Working Group adopted a working definition of middle
;hborhoods as places that are (a) at risk of decline; (b) have modest/median
sing values and household incomes; (c) may be overlooked in definitions of
s as consisting of two classes (rich and poor), and (d) are places where assets
underleveraged.

group turned its attention to the characteristics of middle neighborhoods,
.ng that these neighborhoods may be places where one group of people
res to leave and another market segment aspires to move in. The future of
dle neighborhoods is likely to be affected by the quality of public services, the
ence or absence of local institutions, and the degree of social capital in the
dle neighborhoods—all of which needs careful research.

e practically, the group discussed the need to use research to make the case
the value of middle neighborhoods, seeking to measure the costs associated
i the decline of middle neighborhoods, including the decline in tax base; and
benefits to sustaining the well-being of this class of neighborhoods, including
efficient use of built infrastructure, the opportunity for upward mobility of
dren living in functional neighborhoods, and the value inherent in the
rsity of these areas.

EARCH TO INFORM POLICY

earch is needed that looks at middle neighborhoods in strong and weak market
ros in order to characterize the policy approaches needed in both of these
ket settings. While this research needs to be regional in scope, a careful look
eded at the neighborhood level to capture more localized issues, such as the
cts of foreclosures on middle neighborhoods. Middle neighborhoods are not
a big city phenomenon, as they exist in suburbs also, especially older suburbs
i modest housing styles. Policy approaches need to be aimed at both cities
suburbs. As middle neighborhoods are researched, an intermediate step may
eeded, vis-á-vis understanding the dynamics of neighborhood change more

broadly nationally and regionally. Seeing to it that this research is an accu[rate] portrayal of middle neighborhood conditions, may mean that new data sets n[eed] be created, which are not solely based on census tracts.

RESEARCH TO INFORM PRACTICE

Research is needed to help practitioners understand how to slow dowr[n and] reverse downward trajectories for middle neighborhoods. This includes a n[ore] precise understanding of the tipping point factors in middle neighborhoods, [and] their drivers. This could involve providing practitioners with key indicator[s to] map conditions in middle neighborhoods as a way of helping them trace [these] neighborhoods' trajectories. These indicators are not only housing ma[rket] conditions, as they are an effect of perceptions and realities of quality of lif[e in] neighborhoods, including quality of schools and levels of public safety. This [type] of research needs to be localized, as national data sets are not sufficiently nuar[ced] to describe the conditions and trajectories in the many middle neighborho[ods] in the nation. This localized research needs to capture political, social [and] economic data, not only neighborhood market data. Once at this level, rese[arch] can distinguish between causal factors in neighborhood change and more sir[nple] characterizations of neighborhoods. And, the analysis needs to go bey[ond] customary measurements, to include future threats, such as climate change, [the] national political context, economic dislocation, the decline in African-Amer[ican] homeownership, and job instability.

A FORWARD-LOOKING RESEARCH AGENDA

Taking a case study approach may be the most practical and accurate [way] to understanding the diversity of middle neighborhoods and their fu[ture] trajectories. Case studies should have a hypotheses and theory of change bel[hind] them. Research should look at specific middle neighborhoods and ask how [did] they get where they are and what strategies may or may not have worke[d to] protect them. Perhaps these case studies could pair similar neighborhood[s to] further understand the nuances in approach that fit particular circumstar[ces.] Getting at a national view of how many middle neighborhoods are gene[rally] stable, how many are in danger of decline, and how many are threatened [by] gentrification would be of value.

This case study approach should be both quantitative and qualitative and sh[ould] be used to make the case for strengthening middle neighborhoods and to pro[vide] guidance to practitioners on best practices, including successful approache[s to] fundraising, developing coalitions, and establishing political will.

ocating for and conducting research on middle neighborhoods must reckon
the fact that most foundations in the nation are concerned with the poorest
hborhoods, and the connection between middle neighborhoods and the
essed neighborhoods must be made. Perhaps framing middle neighborhoods
opportunity neighborhoods" could help this connection and be understood
hilanthropy. Particular attention should be paid to measuring gain and loss of
sehold wealth in these neighborhoods. Helping to place these neighborhoods
nclusive economic growth discussions at the regional level may also help
light their importance to cities, suburbs, and regions.

summary, the researchers present focused on the need to move the
erstanding of middle neighborhoods to a dynamic one—much more needs
e understood about the trajectories of existing middle neighborhoods. What
dle neighborhoods are threatened with decline? Which are likely to be affected
scalating prices, moving them from affordable to modest income households
riced only for households that have higher incomes? This examination should
ide suburban areas as well as central city neighborhoods as, it appears that
y older suburbs are also encountering the perils of decline or gentrification,
this phenomenon needs to be understood more thoroughly.

ddition to the above, research is needed to understand the forces that lead
dle neighborhoods to hit a tipping point into decline or gentrification and to
er understand what can be done to prevent such these tipping points from
g reached. The research should not only look at middle neighborhood from
istoric perspective, but with a future lens as well. Future threats to middle
hborhoods that include climate change, national political choices, economic
cation, and instability should also be examined.

AGENDA

November 15–16, 2017

WEDNESDAY, NOVEMBER 15, 2017
THE MOTOR HOUSE, BALTIMORE, MD

2:00–4:00 PM	Tour of Baltimore's middle neighborhoods with Healthy Neighborhoods Inc. and community leaders • Belair-Edison • Reservoir Hill
4:00–4:15 PM	Welcome by Paul Brophy
4:15–4:30 PM	The Vision for Baltimore: Neighborhood and Community Prior Mayor Catherine E. Pugh
4:30–5:20 PM	Panel Discussion: Making the Case for a National Neighborhood Movement • Johnette Richardson, Executive Director of Belair-Edison Neighborhoods • Councilwoman Cherelle Parker, Philadelphia City Council • Laura Gamble, Laura Gamble, President of Maryland Regional, PNC Financial Services Moderator: David Erickson, Federal Reserve Bank of San Franc
5:20–5:30 PM	Concluding Remarks Mark Sissman, President of Healthy Neighborhoods Inc.
5:30–7:00 PM	Cocktail Reception
7:30–9:30 PM	Dinner for working group participants

–8:30 AM	Registration and Breakfast
–8:50 AM	Opening Plenary: Agenda and Meeting Goals
–9:10 AM	Grounding Action through Practice Presentations by practitioners on middle neighborhood interventions with research and policy implications • Nedra Sims Fears, Greater Chatham Initiative • Jeffrey Verespej, Old Brooklyn CDC Joel Ratner, Cleveland Neighborhood Progress
–10:00 AM	Open Discussion • Identify the top policy, practice, and research issues
)–11:00 AM	Session I (3 separate discussion groups) • Research Working Group Co-chairs: Todd Swanstrom and Alan Mallach • Practice Working Group Co-chairs: Marcia Nedland and Nedra Sims Fears • Policy Working Group Co-chairs: Joe McNeely and Cherelle Parker
) AM–12:00 PM	Session II (3 separate discussion groups)
)–1:00 PM	Lunch: Communication Goals and Framing
–2:00 PM	Session III (3 separate discussion groups)
–2:30 PM	Coffee break / Co-chairs and Rapporteurs meet
–4:30 PM	Concluding Plenary • Meeting summary • Priorities for moving forward • Aligning action across policy, practice, and research • Next steps
PM	Adjourn

LIST OF PARTICIPANTS

PROJECT DIRECTOR

Paul Brophy
Principal, Brophy & Reilly LLC
Senior Adviser, The American Assembly
New York, NY

HONORABLE GUESTS

Rep. Dwight Evans (D)
Pennsylvania's 2nd District

Rep. Daniel Kildee (D)
Michigan's 5th District

RESEARCH WORKING GROUP

Alan Mallach*
Senior Fellow
Center for Community Progress
Washington, D.C.

Todd Swanstrom*
Professor
Department of Political Science
University of Missouri-St. Louis
St. Louis, MO

Jessie Grogan**
Senior Policy Analyst
Lincoln Institute of Land Policy
Cambridge, MA

Erin Graves
Director of Research
Federal Reserve Bank of Boston
Boston, MA

Jody Landers
Real Estate Agent & Consultant
Greater Lauraville Healthy Neighborhoods
Baltimore, MD

Kendra Parlock
Director
Mayor's Office of Sustainable Solutions
Baltimore, MD

Rolf Pendall
Co-Director
Metropolitan Housing Communities
& Policy Center, Urban Institute
Washington, D.C.

Jacob Rosch
Research Associate
The Reinvestment Fund
Philadelphia, PA

Ed Rutkowski
Founder, Patterson Park CDC
Baltimore, MD

Bob Weissbourd
President
RW Ventures, LLC
Chicago, IL

PRACTICE WORKING GROUP

Nedra Sims Fears*
Executive Director
Greater Chatham Initiative
Chicago, IL

Marcia Nedland*
Principal, Fall Creek Consultants
Ithaca, NY

Stephanie Sung**
Deputy Director of Urban Policy
The American Assembly
New York, NY

Barbara Aylesworth
Senior Program Officer
Healthy Neighborhoods, Inc.
Baltimore, MD

Isabel Barrios
Program Officer
Greater New Orleans Foundation
New Orleans, LA

id Boehlke
nding Member
lthy Neighborhoods Group
hington, D.C.

l Cleary
using Coordinator
ervoir Hill Improvement Council
imore, MD

rlie Duff
ident
lee Baltimore, Inc.
imore, MD

ia Kitsuse
ctor
er Industrial Cities Program,
Funders Network for Smart
wth and Livable Communities
al Gables, FL

Eric Lee
ctor
ghborhood Programs,
ng City Baltimore
imore, MD

O'Neill
ociate Program Officer
erican Cities Practice,
Kresge Foundation
MI

Ratner
ident
eland Neighborhood Progress
eland, OH

ette Richardson
cutive Director
ar-Edison Neighborhoods, Inc.
more, MD

ene Russell
or Program Officer
ter Milwaukee Foundation
aukee, WI

Mike Schubert
Principal
Community Development Strategies
Chicago, IL

Michael Seipp
Executive Director
Southwest Partnership
Baltimore, MD

Paul Singh
Senior Director
Community Initiatives
NeighborWorks America
Washington, D.C.

Séson Taylor-Campbell
Relationship Manager II
PNC Bank
Baltimore, MD

Kyasha Tyson
Director of Economic &
Community Development
Councilwoman Cherelle L. Parker
Philadelphia, PA

Jeffrey Verespej
Executive Director
Old Brooklyn CDC
Cleveland, OH

POLICY WORKING GROUP

Joseph McNeely*
President
McNeely Legal Services
Baltimore, MD

Cherelle Parker*
City Councilwoman, District 9
Philadelphia City Council
Philadelphia, PA

Peter Dolkart**
Regional Community
Development Manager
Federal Reserve Bank of
Richmond, Baltimore Branch
Baltimore, MD

Michael Braverman
Housing Commissioner
Department of Housing and
Community Development
Baltimore, MD

Cathy Califano
First Deputy Director
Department of Planning
and Development
Philadelphia, PA

David Erickson
Director, Community Development
Federal Reserve Bank of San Francisco
San Francisco, CA

Carol Gilbert
Assistant Secretary
Maryland Department of Housing
and Community Development
Baltimore, MD

Dorraine Kirkmire
Manager of Planning
City of Rochester
Rochester, NY

Rachel Meadows
Chief of Staff
Councilwoman Cherelle L. Parker
Philadelphia, PA

Jenaye Munford
Project Manager
Office of City Council President
Philadelphia, PA

Aaron Renn
Senior Fellow
Manhattan Institute
New York, NY

Charles Rutheiser
Senior Associate
Annie E. Casey Foundation
Baltimore, MD

Alison Share
Legislative Counsel
Congressman Dan Kildee
Washington, D.C.

Theresa Singleton
Senior Vice President
Federal Reserve Bank of Philadelphia
Philadelphia, PA

Mark Sissman
President
Healthy Neighborhoods, Inc.
Baltimore, MD

Sam Storey
Community Development
Research Analyst
Federal Reserve Bank of Richmond
Baltimore, MD

Frank Woodruff
Executive Director
National Alliance of Community
Economic Development Associations
Washington, D.C.

OBSERVERS

Nicholas Hamilton
Director of Urban Policy
The American Assembly
New York, NY

David Mortimer
President
The American Assembly
New York, NY

Pamela Puchalski
Principal
Selby Civic Consulting
Senior Advisor
The American Assembly
New York, NY

*   Co-chair   **   Rapporteur

icipants from varying disciplines attended the meeting in Baltimore, each
a familiarity with the context of middle neighborhoods. Efforts were
e to ensure that each working session represented varied expertise among
raphically diverse, small- and medium-sized American cities. Select
ers also joined to offer feedback and guidance about how to align the
lle neighborhood movement with other philanthropic efforts to grow and
lize communities. Imagined initially as three small groups of 8–10 people
ussing issues specific to the three priority areas, the meeting quickly became
subscribed, particularly in the practice group.

agenda for the meeting was developed with substantial contributions by
ers from each working group. Through a series of conference calls, each group
ded how to structure the plenary sessions and working groups to achieve
ific goals. Additional preparatory materials for each working group were
loped and circulated in advance to ensure that the meeting in Baltimore
n with a shared understanding about goals.

overall two-day agenda was structured as follows:

NESDAY, NOVEMBER 15, 2017

of-town participants joined a tour organized by Healthy Neighborhoods,
to gather insights and firsthand evidence of Baltimore's efforts to stabilize
lle neighborhoods. Following the tour, approximately eighty guests comprised
orking group participants and leaders driving the middle neighborhood
ement in Baltimore gathered at a middle neighborhood community facility,
Motor House. Paul Brophy welcomed the group and provided an overview

of the middle neighborhood movement and the need for national neighborh
strategies. Baltimore City Mayor Catherine E. Pugh then welcomed the audie
and described her administration's priorities for neighborhood stabilizat
A panel discussion focused on incentives for private investment in mic
neighborhoods as well as the steps taken in Baltimore and Philadelphia
address both hot and weak market conditions. A reception followed the pa
Afterwards, a dinner for the out-of-town participants and select leaders fi
Baltimore provided an opportunity for sharing experiences and motivations
continuing work in middle neighborhoods.

THURSDAY, NOVEMBER 16, 2017

Fifty-four participants gathered at the Federal Reserve Bank of Richmo
Baltimore offices for a full-day working session. Following an opening plenary c
breakfast, practitioners from Chicago and Cleveland made brief presentati
about efforts to stabilize their cities' middle neighborhoods. The co-chairs for
three sessions then led a plenary discussion about priority issues. Participants t
broke into their working groups led by co-chairs and supported by a rappor
who documented the discussions in detailed notes, with particular attentio
new, innovative ideas and consensus about how to move forward. Over lui
participants shared priorities for communication needs. During the conclud
plenary session, each group reported out on recommendations and next s
with feedback from all participants. Congressman Dwight Evans (D-PA) off
closing remarks, emphasizing the need for coordinated action and leaders
Following the meeting's adjournment, a concluding dinner brought the leader
of the middle neighborhoods working groups together with Congressman Dw
Evans (D-PA), Congressman Dan Kildee (D-MI) and their staffs to discuss
to build on the momentum of the emerging middle neighborhood movem
including implementation of specific takeaways from the meeting.

THE BALTIMORE BRANCH OF THE FEDERAL RESERVE BANK OF RICHMOND

The Federal Reserve Bank of Richmond is one of twelve regional Reserve B[...] working together with the Board of Governors to foster economic stability [...] strength. It serves in the Fifth Federal Reserve District, including the Caroli[...] Maryland, Virginia, most of West Virginia and our nation's capital. The Richm[...] Fed works to help people be more confident in their financial decisions and in[...] nation's economic and financial systems. They do this by helping the econom[...] by promoting stable prices, employment and moderate long-term interest r[...] working to ensure a safe and sound financial system; and connecting with t[...] District's community and business leaders. The Community Developm[...] department at the Richmond Fed works with local stakeholders and part[...] to identify and address economic impediments and opportunities in low-[...] moderate-income communities in the Fifth District.

LINCOLN INSTITUTE OF LAND POLICY

The Lincoln Institute of Land Policy seeks to improve quality of life through the effe[...] use, taxation, and stewardship of land. A nonprofit private operating founda[...] whose origins date to 1946, the Lincoln Institute researches and recommends cre[...] approaches to land as a solution to economic, social, and environmental challe[...] Through education, training, publications, and events, Lincoln Institute integ[...] theory and practice to inform public policy decisions worldwide.

HEALTHY NEIGHBORHOODS, INC.

Healthy Neighborhoods, Inc. ("HNI") is a Baltimore CDFI non-profit suppor[...] organization of the Baltimore Community Foundation. HNI helps strong[...] undervalued neighborhoods increase home values, market their communi[...] create high standards for property improvement and build strong connect[...] among neighbors. HNI work in forty-two Baltimore neighborhoods is b[...] on the following premises: 1) Baltimore competes with surrounding cou[...] for homebuyers; 2) Neighborhood plans must build upon strengths and a[...] of the neighborhood; 3) "Over improving" homes builds value; 4) Incre[...] appreciation and equity is a good thing; and 5) An improved property imp[...] neighbors' property values.

REPORT DESIGN
Elizabeth Nebiolo

COVER IMAGE
Strong City Baltimore